wild, wild world

DINOSAURS
AND OTHER PREHISTORIC REPTILES

Written by
Denny Robson

Illustrated by
James Field

p

This is a Parragon Book
First published in 2001

Parragon
Queen Street House
4 Queen Street
Bath BA1 1HE, UK

Copyright © Parragon 2001

Produced by

David West ☍ Children's Books
7 Princeton Court
55 Felsham Road
Putney
London SW15 1AZ

British Library Cataloguing-in-Publication Data

A catalogue record for this book is available from
the British Library.

ISBN 0-75254-665-1

Printed in Italy

Designers
Jenny Skelly
Aarti Parmar
Illustrator
James Field
(SGA)
Cartoonist
Peter Wilks
(SGA)
Editor
James Pickering
Consultant
Steve Parker

CONTENTS

? What were the dinosaurs?

Dinosaurs were reptiles of many amazing shapes and sizes that lived long ago. They had just the same needs as the animals you know today – to hunt, feed, breed and escape their enemies.

Triassic   Jurassic

Is it true?
Dinosaurs only lived on land.

Yes. They were adapted for life on land because they walked with straight legs tucked underneath their bodies, as we do. This gave them an advantage over other animals and helped them dominate the land.

Herrerasaurus

Where did they live?

Everywhere on Earth, but the planet was completely different in dinosaur times. The seas, plants, animals and continents, Laurasia and Gondwana were all different. And there were no people!

Cretaceous

Laurasia

Gondwana

When did they live?

Dinosaurs ruled the world for millions of years. They appeared about 225 million years ago and died out 65 million years ago. There were three periods in dinosaur history: Triassic, when the first dinosaurs appeared; Jurassic and Cretaceous, when dinosaurs dominated the land.

Amazing! One of the earliest dinosaurs ever found was *Eoraptor*, 'dawn stealer', and it lived 225 million years ago. It was only one metre long and probably a fierce hunter of small reptiles.

Eoraptor

? Were there any other animals?

Insects, small mammals and many modern forms of life lived in the shadow of the dinosaurs, as well as other reptiles. Pterosaurs soared through the air, while ichthyosaurs and plesiosaurs swam in the seas.

Pterosaurs

Plesiosaur

Ichthyosaur

? Where did dinosaurs come from?

There was life on Earth for over 3,000 million years before the dinosaurs. Mammal-like reptiles were living on the land just before the dinosaurs appeared. Some scientists think *Lagosuchus* (which means rabbit crocodile) was the ancestor of all dinosaurs.

Lagosuchus

Amazing! There were many groups of land-based reptiles 245 million years ago. These included crocodile-like animals which grew up to five metres long.

Archaeopteryx

? How do we know that dinosaurs existed?

Scientists called palaeontologists examine dinosaur bones and piece them together. They also study fossilised footprints, nests and eggs, dung and even toothmarks on bones.

Fossils

Lizard

Deltatheridium

Is it true?
We know everything about dinosaurs from fossils.

No. Scientists must guess what colour dinosaurs were, what noises they made and how they behaved. They compare what they know about dinosaurs with the animals alive today.

Hesperorni

Which were the biggest dinosaurs?

In the Jurassic age, giant plant eaters called sauropods became the largest animals to walk on Earth. One of them, *Ultrasauros*, may have been up to 30m long and about 18m high, which is as tall as a six storey building!

Is it true?
All sauropods were huge and wide.

No. Sauropods were huge, but some were 'slim'. This helped when they walked through woods looking for food.

Compsognathus

Which dinosaurs were the smallest?

Compsognathus was the size of a turkey and weighed about three kilograms. It hunted insects and lizards. *Heterodontosaurus* and *Lesothosaurus*, both plant-eating dinosaurs, were just as small.

? Which were the heaviest dinosaurs?

Ultrasauros may have weighed as much as 50 tonnes, but scientists have recently found evidence of an even bigger dinosaur in Argentina. The gigantic *Argentinosaurus* may have weighed as much as 100 tonnes. Most sauropods were smaller, weighing between 30 and 80 tonnes.

Ultrasauros

Amazing! The neck of *Mamenchisaurus* was 15 metres long, strengthened by a system of spines. It could not have been lifted very high. *Mamenchisaurus* probably fed on low growing vegetation.

? How do we know which dinosaurs ate meat, and which ate plants?

We can tell by looking at fossils of their teeth and claws. Meat eaters and plant eaters developed different special features, such as hands that could grasp and grinding or shearing teeth.

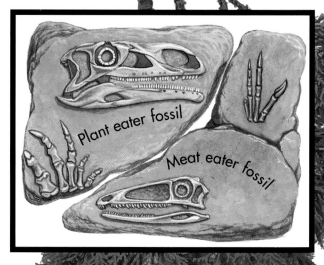

Plant eater fossil

Meat eater fossil

Yunnanosaurus

? What were plant eaters' teeth like?

Yunnanosaurus had chisel-like teeth to cut up tough vegetation. Some sauropods had spoon-shaped teeth for cutting tough plants. Diplodocids had pencil-shaped teeth. They could strip branches bare in seconds by raking leaves through their teeth.

❓ What were meat eaters' teeth and claws like?

Meat eaters such as *Allosaurus* had long, curved, dagger-like teeth to kill and tear at prey. They had powerful jaws in their large heads and strong claws to grip their victims. *Allosaurus* could eat you up in two gulps!

 Is it true?
Some dinosaurs ate stones.

Yes. Plant eaters swallowed stones called gastroliths, to help grind down tough plant food inside their stomachs. Gastroliths were up to ten cm across.

Allosaurus

 Amazing!
Carcharodontosaurus had a huge skull 1.6 metres across, with jaws full of teeth like a shark's. And yet some dinosaurs had no teeth at all! *Gallimimus* fed mainly on insects and tiny creatures it could swallow whole.

11

? Whose teeth were as long as knives?

Tyrannosaurus rex, one of the last dinosaurs, was also one of the largest and fiercest meat eaters ever to live on Earth. Its ferocious teeth were 15 cm long. It used them to strip away flesh while it held its prey down with its feet.

Tenontosaurus

12

Is it true?
Some dinosaurs were cannibals.

Yes. Two skeletons of *Coelophysis* have been found containing the bones of smaller *Coelophysis*. They had eaten the young animals as their last meal.

What would kick out at its prey?

Deinonychus had an enormous slashing claw on each foot. It probably hunted and killed in packs, attacking its prey with a flying leap.

Baryonyx

Deinonychus

Amazing! *Baryonyx* had large, curved claws that may have been used for hooking fish out of water. Its jaw was very similar to the jaws of modern fish-eating crocodiles.

What had a 'terrible hand'?

Deinocheirus means 'terrible hand'. It had hands with long claws which must have been deadly, and arms three metres long. Compared to this, *T. rex*'s arms were tiny!

? What used its tongue like a giraffe's?

Iguanodon used its long tongue to pull leaves into its mouth. On the 'thumb' of each hand it had a defensive spike. When this was first discovered, people thought it was a horn from its nose!

Iguanodon

 Is it true?
Most dinosaurs were peaceful, plant-eating creatures which never attacked anything.

Yes. Most dinosaurs were actually gentle animals, rather than monster killing machines like *Tyrannosaurus Rex*.

Brachiosaurus

? Which dinosaurs travelled in groups?

Fossilised footprints from 80 million years ago tell us that *Brachiosaurus* travelled in herds, like most other plant-eating sauropods. It had huge nostrils, perhaps to smell with, to help cool it, or even to make a noise.

14

Amazing! Huge plant eaters had to eat a huge amount. A *Brachiosaurus* may have eaten a tonne of vegetation a day. It must have spent its whole day walking, eating and producing waste!

Psittacosaurus

What had a beak like a parrot?

Psittacosaurus means 'parrot reptile'. With a narrow, parrot-like beak, strong jaws and sharp teeth, it was able to chew through very tough plants.

? Were huge plant eaters ever attacked?

The sheer size of many of these gentle giants must have put off many predators. Some like *Apatosaurus* had long claws to defend themselves in case they were attacked. They would rear up on their back legs and slash out at their enemies.

Heterodontosaurus

Ceratosaurus

Amazing! Plant eaters like *Heterodontosaurus* had fangs which they may have used to bite attackers. It was a small but strong dinosaur, well able to defend itself against meat eaters.

Is it true?
Scientists can tell how quickly dinosaurs could travel.

Yes. By looking at their skeletons and measuring the distance between fossilised footprints, scientists can measure how quickly or slowly a dinosaur moved.

Apatosaurus

❓ What had spikes at the end of its tail?

The enemies of *Stegosaurus* would have had to watch out for the bony spikes in its tail. Many plant-eating dinosaurs developed spikes, horns or claws to protect themselves from attack.

❓ What could run away from attackers?

Some small plant eaters relied on running away to defend themselves. They would have had good hearing and sharp eyesight. *Dryosaurus* could run at about 40 kph.

Dryosaurus

What whacked its enemies with a club?

The skull and body of *Euoplocephalus* were protected with bony plates, spines and spikes. It also had a huge club at the end of its tail. When attacked, it would swing this club at its enemy.

18

Hylaeosaurus

Euoplocephalus

What wore armour to protect itself?

Many dinosaurs had a thick layer of bony skin which protected them like a suit of armour. *Hylaeosaurus* would lie low to the ground so that its attacker couldn't get under its armour.

Amazing! Another armoured dinosaur, *Huayangosaurus,* had sharp spikes running from its shoulder to the middle of its tail. When it was attacked, it would point the spikes on its back at the enemy and lash out with its tail.

Tyrannosaurus rex

Triceratops

? What had a horn like a rhinoceros?

Triceratops had three large horns, two over its eyes and one on its snout. Its neck and shoulders were protected by a frill of bone. There were many horned dinosaurs, most of which fed together in herds.

❓ Which dinosaurs had 'trumpets'?

Many 'duck-billed' dinosaurs, like *Parasaurolophus*, had strange crests on their heads. The male's crest was much larger than the female's. It was hollow and connected to the nostrils. Perhaps these dinosaurs used their crests like trumpets, making sounds to show off to their mates or to threaten rival males.

 Is it true?
Scientists were the first people to discover dinosaur tracks.

No. Native Americans were using designs which included dinosaur footprints, long before dinosaur tracks were discovered by scientists.

Parasaurolophus

Pachycephalosaurus

Allosaurus

Diplodocus

❓ What used its tail as a whip?

Diplodocus was a huge, plant-eating dinosaur with an enormously long neck and tail. It could measure 27 metres from nose to tail. When it was attacked, it used its tail like a whip, lashing it from side to side.

❓ What used to fight with its head?

Male dinosaurs probably fought for territory and mates, like animals do today. *Pachycephalosaurus* had a skull with a dome of thick bone, like a crash helmet. This was probably to protect its brain during head-butting fights with rivals.

? Did dinosaurs lay eggs?

Yes. Dinosaurs laid eggs, just as reptiles and birds do today. Scientists have found fossil eggs all over the world. Most are empty, but some eggs have been found with the fossil bones of baby dinosaurs inside.

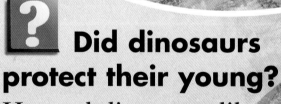

Centrosaurus

? Did dinosaurs protect their young?

Horned dinosaurs like *Centrosaurus* lived in large family groups, like elephants. When threatened, the adults probably surrounded the young, making a frightening wall of horns.

Maiasaura

23

 Amazing! *Oviraptor* was thought to live on stolen eggs, because its skeleton was found on the eggs of another dinosaur. But a baby *Oviraptor* has now been found inside one of the eggs. So scientists can't decide if it's a thief or not!

 Is it true?
Dinosaur eggs were huge.

No. Dinosaur eggs were only about 12 cm long. If they were bigger, the shell would have been too thick for the young to break through.

? Which reptile made nests?

Maiasaura, 'good mother reptile', made nests in groups. Each parent would dig a hollow in the sand, the female would lay up to 25 eggs, then the eggs were covered with plants to keep them warm.

Amazing! The largest lizards ever were mosasaurs, huge reptiles that swam in the sea. They were real sea monsters – ten metres long with huge mouths, and they looked like dragons! They probably ate anything they could catch.

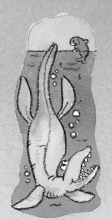

? Were there dinosaurs in the sea?

No. All dinosaurs lived on land, but there was a variety of strange reptiles that swam in the seas in dinosaur times. Ichthyosaurs were strong swimming reptiles that looked like dolphins and could breathe air. They probably hunted in packs, feeding on fish and squid.

Ammonite

Ichthyosaurs

 Is it true?
The Loch Ness Monster exists.

Who knows? People who believe that there really is a monster in Loch Ness think it may well be a plesiosaur. What do you think?

What was all neck?

Plesiosaurs were also swimming reptiles. They had four paddle-like limbs and a tail. *Elasmosaurus* was a long-necked plesiosaur. Its tiny head sat on an amazingly long neck that was half its total length of 13 metres.

Elasmosaurus

Liopleurodon

What had a huge head?

Liopleurodon was one of the short-necked plesiosaurs. But its head was four metres long! It probably fed on shellfish and turtles, crunching them up with dagger-like teeth that were ten centimetres long.

❓ What was the earliest bird?

The earliest bird discovered was *Archaeopteryx*, which lived 150 million years ago. Birds are the dinosaurs' closest living relatives. Some scientists believe they evolved from dinosaurs such as *Deinonychus,* only smaller.

Archaeopteryx

Amazing!
Pterodaustro had a sieve in its beak so that it could strain fish from the water as it flew low over the sea.

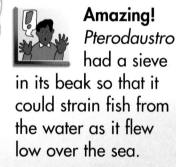

Rhamphorhynchus

❓ Were there flying dinosaurs?

The reptiles gliding through the air weren't dinosaurs but pterosaurs. The earliest pterosaurs were rhamphorhynchids which appeared about 200 million years ago.

❓ **What were pterodactyls?**

Pterodactyls, which means 'wing-finger', were pterosaurs. They were sleek and streamlined, and grew to huge sizes. They had crests on their heads, but no tail and no teeth. They appeared 150 million years ago and died out at the same time as the dinosaurs.

Pterodactylus

Is it true?
Quetzalcoatlus *was bigger than a hang-glider.*

Yes. This huge pterodactyl was the biggest airborne animal that ever lived. It had a wingspan of up to 15 metres.

? Why did the dinosaurs disappear?

Some scientists think it was because a large meteorite hit Earth, or because huge volcanoes erupted and the climate changed. Movement of land and seas meant there were also fewer places for dinosaurs to live. It could be all of these reasons.

Amazing! A huge crater 180 km across has been found on the seabed near Mexico. It was formed 65 million years ago. Could this be from a meteorite that wiped out the dinosaurs?

? Why would a meteorite wipe out the dinosaurs?

When the meteorite hit the surface of the Earth, there would have been a huge explosion. Dust would fill the air, blocking out the Sun's light for several months. Without the Sun vegetation would die, the plant eaters would die, and finally the large meat eaters would starve.

Zalambdalestes

29

? Did all the animals disappear?

No, although many other species died out along with the dinosaurs. These included pterosaurs and marine reptiles such as plesiosaurs. Most bigger animals became extinct. But smaller animals survived, and these creatures evolved in a world without the dinosaur.

How do museums make dinosaur skeletons?

Lots of people are involved, from fossil hunters to people who transport the bones, palaeontologists, laboratory technicians, even artists and photographers. The bones are put together in order and held in place by steel supports.

Is it true?
Artists can help to show what dinosaurs looked like.

Yes. When scientists have identified bones, artists draw what the dinosaur might have looked like when it was alive.

❓ Do museums use real bones?

No. Original fossils are too heavy and valuable. Instead scientists make copies from light-weight materials and keep the real bones safe.

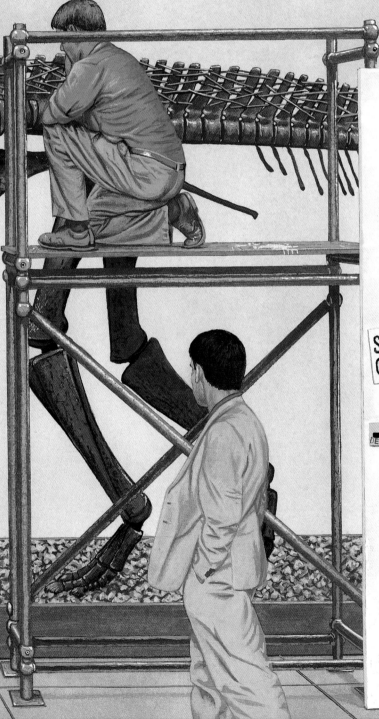

STAFF ONLY

DINO TOUR

Amazing! Scientists think that they might have found a missing link between birds and dinosaurs. *Sinosauropteryx* was a true dinosaur, but it had a feathery covering, and its feet had sharp pointed claws, much like a chicken's.

31

Sinosauropteryx

Glossary

Cretaceous period The third period in dinosaur history, which lasted from 135 million years ago until the extinction of the dinosaurs about 65 million years ago.

Evolution A gradual change in form over many generations.

Extinction When a group of animals or plants dies out.

Fossil The preserved remains of something that was once alive.

Ichthyosaurs Marine reptiles that were alive in dinosaur times.

Jurassic period The second period in dinosaur history, which lasted from 200 – 135 million years ago.

Meteorite A rock which flies through outer space until it lands on Earth, sometimes with disastrous results.

Palaeontologist A person who studies fossilised remains.

Plesiosaurs Marine reptiles with large flippers, which were alive in dinosaur times.

Pterosaurs Reptiles which travelled through the air in prehistoric times.

Sauropods Large plant-eating dinosaurs that included *Diplodocus*.

Triassic period The first period in dinosaur history, which lasted from 225 – 200 million years ago, when the first of the dinosaurs appeared on Earth.

Index